Courtship
THE 21ST CENTURY
PROCESS

It's Classic

It's Honorable

It's Intentional

It's Biblical

Courtship
THE 21ST CENTURY
P R O C E S S

RICKEY E. MACKLIN

Rickey E. Macklin

ISBN 978-1-7351340-0-0 (paperback)
ISBN 978-1-7351340-1-7 (digital)

All Scripture quotations are taken from the Holy Bible, King James Version.

Published by Rickey E. Macklin
Courtshipvsdating.com

Printed in the United States of America

Dedication

This book is dedicated to
the single, divorced, widow, widower,
and those starting over again.
Keep God at the forefront of your relationships,
and everything else
will come into alignment
in His time.

A friend loveth at all times,
and a brother is born for adversity.

– Proverbs 17:17

Healthy relationships should always
begin at the spiritual and intellectual
levels—the levels of purpose, motivation,
interests, dreams, and personality.

– Dr. Myles Munroe

Chivalry in love has nothing to do with
the sweetness of the appearance.
It has everything to do with
the tenderness of a heart
determined to serve.
You must not act under the impetus
of charm, but out of a commitment to
make someone's life
the joy you want it to be.

– Ravi Zacharias

Therefore, shall a man leave his father and his mother, and shall cleave unto his wife: and they shall be one flesh.

– Genesis 2:24

A successful marriage requires falling in love many times, always with the same person.

– Mignon McLaughlin

Marital fidelity means that your spouse's health, happiness, security, and welfare take a higher place in your life than anything else except your own relationship with the Lord.

– Dr. Myles Munroe

Contents

Introduction

For the past twenty years, I have taught classes and spoken at workshops and seminars on the subject of *biblical* courtship. As you can imagine, I get asked a lot of questions. Two of the most frequent ones are:

When are you going to write a book?

Well, that time has finally come! I am excited to offer you this book. In its pages, you will find a synopsis of the courtship process and examples to use as you seek God's guidance in this important journey.

Why are you so passionate about courtship?

The simple answer: I want to help you. I desire to help reduce the statistics of future divorces before the expression "I do" is ever avowed. I want to help you bypass the pitfalls and dangers you so often face when forming relationships. While there is no one plan or process that can guarantee success every time, I truly believe the information provided in this book will point you in the right direction. It will help you develop a happy and healthy relationship and set you on the path to a successful marriage.

As you read this book, I hope you catch a glimpse of why I am so passionate about courtship. I pray this book answers your questions about relationships, helps you build confidence as you seek your mate, and reveals the ultimate expression of God's relationship with the Church. It outlines the basics and offers sound advice on how to navigate courtship in the twenty-first century.

As you enjoy this journey, remember:

COURTSHIP
Classic • Honorable • Intentional • Biblical

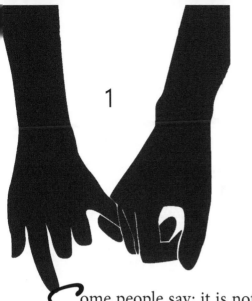

THE BASICS

*S*ome people say: it is not how you start, but how you finish that counts. I say: how you start a relationship has a lot to do with its success or failure.

Although the process of courting is essential, it is not as essential as how we *start* the courting process. How we choose a mate is critical to the success of the relationship.

In biblical times, family was the first institution God created through the marital union of Adam and Eve. God said it was not good that man should be alone, so He made Adam a "helpmeet," Eve. She was made to assist Adam in his God-given assignment. With all of the amazing gifts Eve had, her purpose was not to serve Adam but to help him. As you may have noticed, the prerequisite to this union was not love but purpose.

Later in biblical history, family alliances were made based upon property and bloodlines. The idea of marriage being of friendship and love were developed later.

During the Middle Ages and the Victorian era, mate selection was still a pragmatic decision. The upper-class married for political and economic reasons while the lower classes had more flexibility in choosing mates.

I do not particularly agree with the method of parents choosing their children's mates, especially in cases where the couple has had no prior interaction, but I can see the benefits of having emotional security and financial stability throughout the process.

One major development over the past century has been the introduction of romantic love, chemistry, and sexual compatibility as priorities in choosing a mate.

I understand that no one wants a loveless or sexless marriage, and I am in no way suggesting that you marry anyone you do not love. However, as the late Dr. Myles Monroe stated, *"Purpose is the key to fulfillment. Where purpose is unknown, abuse is inevitable."*

What Is the Purpose of Marriage?

The purpose of marriage, as defined in God's eyes, is not sex, having amazing chemistry, or finding romantic love. The purpose of marriage, beyond procreation, is to fulfill God's mission together with your partner and show the world a picture of God's love through the demonstration of love towards one another. Marriage provides a glimpse of the union that will one day take place between Christ and His Church.

The PURPOSE *of* MARRIAGE *is* **NOT sex**.

Should you love the person you plan to marry? Yes, of course. Should you have an attraction to the person you plan to marry? Yes, of course. However, these things pale in comparison to having a mate who is in sync with you, who complements you, and who can assist you in fulfilling your God-given purpose.

Here is a quote I find befitting:

Much of the customs of courtship during the Colonial times revolved around rational needs and not lust. A man was only able to marry when he could support a family with his income and possessions. Many believed that love developed only after a marriage progressed and not before. Nevertheless, this quickly changed during the 1800s when love started to become important. The love referred to, however, was not romantic love for romantic love was seen as childish. Instead, couples sought openness and sincerity in a mate. (Cate & Lloyd, 1992.)

What is Courting?

Merriam-Webster's Dictionary defines "**to court**" as: "to seek to gain; to seek to win a pledge of marriage from; to engage in social activities leading to engagement and marriage." From this definition alone, you can see how courting is a serious activity. It implies mutual exclusivity, not an open relationship with multiple options.

Courtship is classic, honorable, intentional, and it is biblical. Allow me to address these attributes here.

It Is Classic

Courtship transcends ordinary relationships and has a timeless quality. Some would even say it is vintage and old-fashioned, but it has time-honored traditions that endure and have the most lasting results. Some might consider Ford Model T's a classic or some vinyl records rare, but I think of my parents' fifty-five-year marriage. To me, that is as classic and rare as it gets.

My parents met while they were working together in Queens, New York. They began their courtship one month after meeting, and they married seven months later. They moved to my mother's hometown in Camden, South Carolina, where they remained for the entirety of *For both of them,* **DIVORCE** *was* **NEVER** *an* **OPTION**. their fifty-five-year marriage. For the both of them, divorce was never an option. While no marriage is perfect, God provided a grace that enabled them to endure trials and persevere through storms, resulting in a beautiful legacy that kept God first. Courtship is classic.

It Is Honorable

In courtship, the relationship is carried out in a morally upright and principled manner. Couples carefully make decisions together, keeping in mind the heart and needs of their mates. Each party is conscious of their speech, whether it is temperate or demeaning.

IT IS A RELATIONSHIP PREGNANT WITH FOCUSED INTENTION.

Each makes the other an intentional priority. Whether in each other's presence or apart, each party in the courtship exhibit actions that exemplify how much he or she esteems and honors his or her mate. Courtship is honorable.

IT IS INTENTIONAL

Successful courtship requires actions that are purposeful and deliberate. It is a relationship pregnant with focused intention. In courtship, when a gentleman approaches a lady, he does it with the hope that she is the one he will one day marry. When the lady accepts the pursuit, she accepts with the hope that the gentleman pursuing her is the one she will one day marry. While a great deal of events take place between the first meeting and marriage and there is a chance the relationship may not result in marriage, the objective is still clear. With courtship, there is not any period in which either party engages with a person with no real commitment and no direction on where things will end up. Courtship is intentional.

IT IS BIBLICAL

The one comment that I have heard a lot is that court-ship does not appear in the Bible, so how can it be biblical? Courtship is biblical because it prioritizes the union of marriage, which is a preview of the relationship between Christ and His Church. Because of this significance, the courtship process is carried out with the highest form of character.

Courtship *is a* HIGHER LEVEL *of* **training** *on* OPERATING *in the* PUREST FORM *of* **Love**.

You and your prospective mate must walk through the courtship process in a way that pleases God. Consider the feelings of your prospective mate before your own. You must establish a trust through consistency. Allow the other person in the relationship to feel protected and secure. A successful courtship is an exercise of restraint and selflessness. You must be careful not to awaken deeper feelings before it is time, which is different from regular relationship development, which, at times, puts the self at the forefront. Although courtship focuses on purpose and intent, it is also a higher level of training for operating with the purest form of love.

Remember:

- Love perseveres patiently and doesn't lose heart.

- Love is slow to anger and slow to avenge.

- Love is kind and mild-mannered.

- Love does not covet and is not moved by envy or jealousy over another.

- Love does not boast or brag.

- Love does not display itself haughtily.

- Love is not puffed up or conceited.

- Love is not arrogant and inflated with pride.

- Love does not act unbecomingly or disgracefully.

- Love does not seek, or place demands on others. It does not strive for recognition. It considers others first. It is unselfish.

- Love is not easily provoked, irritated, or aroused to anger. It possesses grace for others.

- Love does not think evil. Although evil may exist, love does not impute it to others.

- Love is not happy or joyful at another's unjust treatment. However, it does happily rejoice with all things considered right and true.

- Love bears all things that are borne with a good conscience. It covers with silence the errors and the faults of others.

- Love is ever ready to believe the best in a person and to place confidence in him or her without suspicion.

- Love keeps hope alive. Even against hope, it keeps believing what is good of another even when others have ceased to do so.

- Love's hope does not fade, no matter the circumstances.

- Love endures all things. Whether faced with persecutions, distresses, or misfortunes, it shows an affectionate spirit to the other person.

- Love never ceases, never passes away, and is never rendered ineffective. Love never fails.

While we have spoken extensively on love, we should also take a look at the other aspects of the fruit of the Spirit, because a properly executed courtship will develop all of them.

- There should be joy, cheerfulness, delight, and gladness. Those in the relationship will exhibit stability and calmness in their dealings with one another. They should be glad to see and experience each other, no matter what the circumstance.

- There should be peace and harmony between individuals in a relationship. Peace and harmony make and keep things safe and prosperous. They develop the union by allowing the couple to walk together, make decisions together, and start to develop the oneness that the marriage union creates.

- Both participants in a relationship should be long-suffering towards one another. This involves patience, endurance, constancy, steadfastness, and perseverance, especially while bearing troubles and ills.

- Both participants in a relationship should exercise gentleness, goodness, and kindness toward each other and to others, both individually and as a couple.

- Both partners should display faith and fidelity toward God first and each other second.

- Both partners should display meekness, humility, and mildness.

- Both partners should practice temperance in place of temptations, and exercise self-control. Temperance is the virtue of one who masters his or her desires and passions, especially sensual appetites.

What Is the Result of Courtship?

Lastly, because the end result is marriage, the courtship process will assist the couple in operating in their God-ordained positions in the family. Biblical courtship, at its fundamental source, is the preparation for marriage as God intended. By their experiences and purposed interactions during courtship, the lady will learn the biblical concept of reverencing her husband while the gentleman learns to love his wife so deeply that he is willing, if need be, to sacrifice his life for hers. Because the lady experiences the depth of the gentleman's love, she will desire to revere him and willingly subject herself to a husband who loves and honors her and has a vision and purpose for himself and the family. See Ephesians 5:22–33 and Galatians 5:22–23. Courtship is biblical.

What are the Benefits of Courtship?

There are three benefits of courtship—Real Commitment, Security, and Accountability.

Real Commitment

There is no courtship without intentionality and commitment. If you are not ready to commit to a lasting relationship, you are not ready to court. While dating, a person may string you along for years with empty promises and no assurance, but courtship requires true commitment from each person. Commitment in courtship is your dedication, faithfulness, and loyalty to the decision that you have made to the other person. Courtship gives you an unspoken and an unwavering assurance. Since courtship offers this wonderful benefit of commitment, the ability to work through the difficult times is woven into the framework of the relationship. It enables both of you to face challenges instead of walking away.

SECURITY

Proper courtship fortifies trust, relieves insecurities, and focuses attention on serving each other. Courtship stands guard over the relationship and protects the heart and the vulnerabilities of your mate. This security creates a safe environment through consistency, which allows the couple to genuinely get to know one another.

In courtship, you are intentionally taking the risk of sharing your visions, missions, and dreams with someone else. Because of the commitment made to one another, courtship

Courtship

allows both of you to share in the relationship without anxiety, fear, or reservation.

ACCOUNTABILITY

Accountability is the obligation or willingness to accept responsibility for one's actions. For accountability in a relationship to work, both partners must be vulnerable, honest, trusting, and transparent.

The article "Relationships and Accountability" by Jason Lauritsen is a great resource for accountability. The information from the article will assist you in understanding what accountability in the courtship relationship involves. Here is an excerpt:

RELATIONSHIPS AND ACCOUNTABILITY

"Accountability in a relationship of any type requires these basic things:

- Clear expectations. You can't live up to expectations you aren't aware of or that you don't understand.

- Communication. Being in an ongoing conversation about how things are going and what is changing is critical. These conversations produce feedback about how things are going and provide the opportunity to learn and adapt.

- Commitment. Being accountable in the relationship means that you will sometimes need to do things that you don't want to do or could get away without doing. You do these things willingly for one another." (Lauritsen, 2018.)

In courtship, there are two forms of accountability, external and internal.

External is typically established between close friends, mentors, or spiritual leaders. In this type of relationship, you communicate your relational dreams and desires with someone and agree that it is okay for that person to hold you accountable. This person will have a vested interest in seeing you reach your goals. They are not judgmental.

They will act as a guardrail to help keep you focused and on track with your dreams. **Internal** is the most important accountability relationship to establish between the courting couple. Here, you are potentially establishing a relationship with a lifetime partner. As with external accountability relationships, an internal relationship requires vulnerability, honesty, trust, and transparency. In courtship, you both are accountable to each other. You are accountable for what you have communicated to each other and agreed upon, while also adhering to the standards and boundaries the two of you both have set in the relationship.

They will have JUST ENOUGH **grace** *for you.*

The main benefit of accountability is freedom. In a trusting relationship, it is okay to show your flaws and it is understood that neither party is perfect. The person you are with is in your life to help you become better. They will have grace for your struggles, for your mistakes, and for your shortcomings. They will have enough to forgive you and enough to keep right on loving you. In this mutually committed relationship, your prospective mate will help you own your mistakes but will not make you deal with them alone.

Where no counsel is, the people fall: but in the multitude of counselors there is safety.

–Proverbs 11:14

Courtship

My key takeaways for this chapter

_____

_____

_____

_____

_____

_____

_____

_____

_____

_____

_____

_____

_____

_____

_____

_____

_____

JOYFUL COURTERS TELL ALL

∽

Your CourtshipVsDating Facebook and Instagram pages have had a tremendous impact in my everyday life. I've gotten a lot out of them and I know many others have too. Keep doing what you're doing because it's helped change my life in ways I couldn't even explain."

~ Stacie Bell

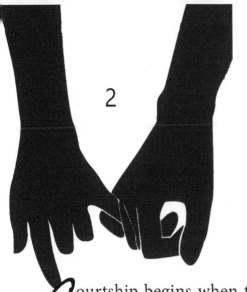

2

THE PROCESS

*C*ourtship begins when the *man* pledges a commitment and the *woman* accepts it. Please note that the pursuit and wooing start before courtship begins. To be clear, the wooing in the relationship should never stop and continue deep into the marriage.

This assumes four things:

- Both the pursuer and the pursued have a clear understanding of who they are, their purpose in life, their core values, and the intricacies of courtship.

- Both have established an intimate relationship with God first. This vertical relationship with God enables them to have a loving relationship with each other.

- Before the man pursues the woman, he has sought God concerning his motives in the pursuit. Once he has, he then pursues her in a deliberate and intentional way.

- Before the woman accepts the pursuit, she has sought God concerning her motives in allowing the pursuit.

Observing a woman from a distance is great, as is befriending her. But before a man begins his pursuit of a woman, he should seek God about it. I am certain he does not want to waste time and neither does she.

Investing in **prayer first** *will save* **time, money,** *and result in* **less headaches**..

As a woman, you may feel like these instructions are for you to speak with God and then twiddle your thumbs until a faithful man approaches you. This is far from the truth. While it is true, biblically speaking, the man is the pursuer, you are not sitting idly waiting. Other than preparing yourself for marriage, you should be focusing on your purpose and aspirations. You should be pursing your goals, becoming your best, and achieving everything God equipped you to accomplish. What you attain in your singleness will be a great asset in your marriage later.

Some may say my method is too serious. I believe that broken hearts, abusive relationships, and failed marriages are just as serious as my method. My objective is to assist in making healthy and happy relationships and to prevent broken marriages before couples say, "I do." Marriage is for the mature. If you are not ready for marriage, do not enter into courtship.

I am not suggesting you meet them today and start courting tomorrow. Nor am I suggesting you follow the strict, Victorian-era guidelines of courtship when a lady was never permitted to go out alone to meet a gentleman. She could never address a gentleman without an introduction. There was no physical contact between the lady and the gentleman before marriage. Additionally, even if she entered the stage of courtship, she could never walk with the gentleman. What I am suggesting is that you approach relationships from a different perspective.

For men, it is important that you are clear regarding your intentions. Women are attracted to men who are upfront in going after what they want. However, telling someone you just met for the first time, *"I am going to marry you,"* may indicate honesty on your part, but it may also scare a woman away.

Having said that, there are exceptions to this. When you know that you are being led by God, be courageous in sharing what He has placed on your heart. I recall hearing the story of my late Bishop and his wife. Originally from North Carolina, he met his wife for the first time in Washington, DC. He told her he knew that she was going to be his wife because God showed him a picture of his wife when he was young, and that picture was of her. Of course, she laughed at the idea. In her mind, she was not going to marry that country boy. They did eventually marry and built a wonderful ministry together.

Nevertheless, your *intent*, as well as the intent of your prospective mate, should be to establish a meaningful relationship that leads to marriage. I strongly encourage you to invest a significant amount of time in the beginning stages of a relationship conversing about these intentions instead of just hanging out. Avoid compromising situations and be intentional with your conversations by talking about things that really matter. While you don't have to treat these conversations as a job interview, you should cover your core values and your non-negotiables. After speaking to one another, you will discover who will and will not meet your long-term needs.

You are simply collecting data *to make a* **sound, reasonable,** *and* **prayed-about** decision.

An example:

You engage in a conversation with someone that you have met at an event, work, or a church outing. After exchanging phone numbers, you begin talking.

After a week or two of conversing on the phone, you decide to meet in person at a coffee shop. I do not recommend going to the movies. You are not going to learn anything beyond whether or not your prospective mate likes butter on their popcorn. All of this is before courtship officially starts because you are simply collecting data to make a sound, reasonable, and prayerful decision. Do not be afraid to ask tough questions.

Note: I do not suggest meeting someone and immediately start planning a night out on the town. If you wanted to just date and get out of the house to quell your loneliness, I could see you going down that path. However, this is courtship we are talking about, not dating.

Guidance for Your First Outing

- Do not act like you are entitled. Be gracious.
- Do not brag about yourself. That is a turn off.
- Do not come on too strong. It shows desperation.
- Do not complain about things. That is a turn off as well.
- Do not talk about your past relationships—unless you are specifically asked.
- Now, relax, enjoy, and be yourself.

If you are feeling a connection after a few meetings that goes beyond physical chemistry and unites with your purpose, then you are on track to move forward with something meaningful.

I do not believe in just hanging out and seeing where things go or letting the chips fall where they may. Sure, things should progress organically but not after months of dating and exposing your heart with no commitment. The beginning is the most critical stage because it sets the foundation for what happens next and further into the relationship, should you start one.

THE IMPORTANCE OF PRAYER

As a believer in Christ, I am convinced that before allowing any emotional connections, romance, pet names, or intimacy to occur, you should seek God about this person and situation.

Yes, I mean you should pray about it.

You pray about almost all other major decisions. Why not this one? Remember, this could impact the rest of your life.

Pray for wisdom. Pray for discernment. Pray for understanding. Pray for clarity. Pray to hear God's voice for instructions on what decision to make. Pray to have your emotions calmed so that you do not move forward out of fear or loneliness.

Additionally, if you are unable to hear from God and you have not received any peace regarding the person, you may want to add fasting with your prayers. If you can do this in collaboration with the person you're interested in, even better! Also, please do not neglect the advice of your accountability partner. Share what you have learned early on and ask for their thoughts and wisdom. Lastly, remember that nothing permanently good comes out of a relationship when you compromise your Godly standards.

How Long Before You Two Should Start Courting?

I hear all the time that it is necessary to spend a lot of time with a person to get to know him or her. For some couples, six months or even a year might be necessary before getting serious. I personally don't support this train of thought. In many cases, after three months, even if you have not already given your body to the other person, you may have still given too much. Maybe you have given your mind, your emotions, and some of you even your money without any form of commitment from them. Soul-ties are not just formed sexually. Logically, it makes sense to spend an enormous amount of time together, but emotionally, you have no protection. If this sounds like dating to you, guess what? It is. You are exposed and in danger of being severely hurt.

SEEK GOD FOR CLARITY

I suggest you should spend more time with God to gain clarity. You do not need to spend months with your prospective mate to see if he or she is a wolf in sheep's clothing. What you need is discernment and wisdom from God. He has a way of disclosing counterfeits and exposing liars. You need to know if the one you are interested in matches your purpose and assignment in life. Even after all their complimenting, you need to know whether he or she complements you as well. God will help those who seek His will to find the mate He has chosen for them.

Make sure you choose someone who is not only built to handle where you are going, but also built to embrace what you have already been through. Not everyone will qualify.

Meeting Potential Mates Online

For those pursuing relationships online, I offer this advice from my book, *Real Talk Relationship Tips.*

Everything in life has a timestamp attached to it. So should the amount of time you invest before meeting the person. Do not allow your social communications of direct messaging and video chatting become a substitute for reality. In other words, plan to meet face-to-face before you become emotionally attached. My personal suggestion is to meet in person before you make a relational commitment.

When you do finally agree to meet, make sure you take precautions to maintain your safety. Always meet in a public setting—preferably during the daytime. Be sure to share their personal information and your plans with a friend or family member. Regardless of what has been expressed on the phone or how you may have felt, meeting them in person will be the teller of truth. If after meeting him or her you are just not feeling it, please be honest with them and let them know. Meeting someone online requires even more prayer, discernment, and patience than meeting someone in person.

STARTING THE COURTSHIP PROCESS

Once you both have peace from God and wise counsel from your accountability partners or mentors, it is time to start the courtship process. Courtship does not mean you are married. Yes, you should respect the relationship and the person you are with. However, no one should be dictating or controlling where you can go and to whom you can talk with. No marital contract has been signed yet. However, because the relationship is exclusive, and marriage is ultimately your intent and goal, a transformation in your mindset must begin.

Set boundaries with those of the opposite sex. Be respectful of your relationship and your mate. Be cognizant of conversations you have with others that you would not want your mate to have with someone else. And please, do not ignore the red flags you see through proper discernment. Don't move forward with someone who has not healed from a past relationship or is still dealing with their insecurities.

Even if it turns out that he or she is not the right one for you and you must break off the relationship, fret not. If you handle the courtship correctly, you may experience some pain in the breakup, but it should not destroy your hope of a future relationship because you honored each other throughout the process.

Do not IGNORE *the flags* **YOU SEE** *through proper* **discernment**.

Ideally, courtship should only happen once, but there are times when we may get it wrong. Do not feel condemned because of it.

MY KEY TAKEAWAYS FOR THIS CHAPTER

_____

_____

_____

_____

_____

_____

_____

_____

_____

_____

_____

_____

_____

_____

_____

_____

_____

JOYFUL COURTERS TELL ALL

∽

"My eyes are wide open now thanks to your biblical teachings on courtship. It's amazing how much the world had me twisted. Now that I know what I know, I will not turn back. I know what God wants for me, and I refuse to settle and have it any other way. I never heard the term "courting" until I came upon your page. A friend of mine liked one of your posts and it showed up in my newsfeed on Facebook. I went directly to your page and fell in love!! It's the truth; it's real talk, and nothing is sugar-coated. I've made many mistakes in the past because of lack of knowledge but now I know the truth. Thanks again for all your hard work and dedication. You are changing lives and in turn, changing our futures!"

~ *France Neptune*

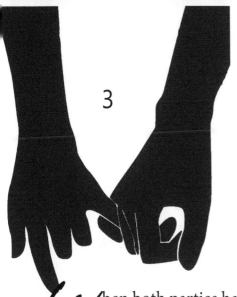

3

THE STAGES

FRIENDSHIP
RELATIONSHIP
ENGAGEMENT

When both parties have agreed to enter into courtship, the process will begin. In this chapter, I will explain the three stages of courtship and help you to understand the importance of each. The significance of these steps is that they fit together and depend on each other.

When you say yes to courtship, you begin by establishing a friendship first, as your relationship will be built upon that foundation. Once the relationship is developed, you will naturally move into the final stage: engagement.

Friendship Stage

While a friendship may exist before courtship begins and is something you can build upon, it is not quite the same as the friendship that is developed in courtship. I always convey to people that you do not have to be friends to start courting each other, but you should be best friends by the time you both say, "I do." You may start the friendship before courtship, but the true friendship is developed in courtship.

How Important Is Friendship?

According to a research paper by Shawn Grover and John F. Helliwell of the National Bureau of Economic Research, couples who are friends have happier marriages. Friendship is a strong mediating factor for the life satisfaction especially when you combine two key life circumstances: marriage and religion. They suggest through their research that while all friends are important for happiness, those who share beliefs (in the Lim and Putnam example) or are married to each other (as in our results) are super-friends, with well-being effects apparently much larger than for friends on average. (Grover, Helliwell, *How Life At Home? New Evidence On Marriage And The Set Point For Happiness,* 2014.)

During this early stage of courtship, you want to build an authentic friendship. Take your time to learn about each other beyond just your physicality. Create a bond that sets the foundation for your relationship and potential marriage. Build this friendship with patience, transparency, kindness, honor, and respect. You will need this later.

There is **no need** *to go quickly from* **zero** *to* **one hundred** *in relationships.*

Build your friendship outside of romance. This is not the time or the season for romance as you are just getting to know the person in the beginning stage of courtship. As Solomon, the wisest man in the Bible except for Christ Jesus, stated, *"Do not stir or awaken love until it pleases" (Song of Solomon 2:7).* In other words, show some restraint and do not arouse emotions that will send the relationship spiraling in a sensual direction that you cannot recover from.

Here is an example of what happens when romance is introduced too quickly in a relationship.

A team of scientists led by Dr. Helen Fisher at Rutgers, concluded that romantic love can be broken down into three categories: lust, attraction, and attachment.

Lust is driven by the desire for sexual gratification. Attraction involves the brain pathways that control "reward" behavior, which partly explains why the first few weeks or months of a relationship can be so exhilarating and even all-consuming.

While lust and attraction are usually exclusive to romantic entanglements, attachment mediates friendships, parent-infant bonding, social cordiality, and many other intimacies as well. (Wu, 2017.)

While attachment is a good thing when building your friendship, take your time and ensure that the attachment is genuine.

Lust, however, is self-seeking and needs to be tempered.

For now, focus on becoming best friends. You will need to agree upon boundaries to maintain your purity. Your integrity will be on the line for how you handle your desires. Protect the relationship *and* protect each other.

One of my mentors, the late Bishop James R. Peebles Sr. (City of Praise Family Ministries/Jericho City of Praise), stated, "Take your time. Move slow. Don't get in a hurry or on the fast track. If it's for you today, it will be for you tomorrow." There is no need to quickly go from zero to one hundred in relationships. You are going to scare people away. Let patience do her perfect work. Whatever God has planned for your life, it cannot be subverted. Indeed, I understand how walking in disobedience can hinder the general blessings that God has in store for us. However, I am specifically speaking to what God has ordained for you. Surely, he will bring it to fruition in His time.

What Can We Do During the Friendship Stage?

While you are courting, focus on your purpose. Focus on having fun, connecting spiritually, becoming financially secure, and helping each other in challenged areas. Focus on the things that really count. Get to know each other's likes, dislikes, strengths, and weaknesses. Here are some ideas for how to do that:

- Take some walks together.
- Attend church together and regularly pray together.
- Play some games and sporting activities together.
- Invest time in getting to know each other's friends and families.
- Plan some day trips. Day trips are perfect for great conversations.
- Visit some museums.
- Go bike riding.
- Do some goal planning together.

- Go to concerts and plays.

- Find an organization where you both can serve others in need.

- Read books on your own and discuss them together.

- Create a scrapbook of the things you do along the way.

- Invest time in learning each other's interests and hobbies.

- Take a finance and communication class together.

- Build an authentic friendship and one day, you'll marry your best friend.

- This list in inexhaustible!

How Should I Handle a Long-Distance Relationship?

Most of these activities should be experienced in person but with the video capabilities we have now, those in a long-distance relationship can still experience things virtually. You can develop strategies and plans, watch movies, work out, attend worship services, go on outings, tour the world, and have game nights. You can do all of these from the comfort of your own home.

Also, please continue to be your authentic self. It can become easy to hide that behind a camera. The good thing about long-distance relationships is that you invest most of your time in communicating, which will help tremendously when you are finally able to be around each other in person.

Just as there is an upside to long-distance relationships, there is a downside as well. For some, this type of relationship is perfect because it helps them manage their physical desires for each other. On the other hand, because you spend less time with each other, there is oftentimes an urgency to fulfill all of your desires when you are finally together. This can be especially hard on couples who are trying to maintain purity.

RELATIONSHIP STAGE

At this stage, some forms of romance may be permissible if they do not lead to you compromising your purity. Your boundaries should not be thrown out the window simply because your relationship has matured, and you have fallen in love. Use your wisdom and remain abstinent until marriage.

The time spent together in this stage is wonderful and should be used to deepen both your spiritual and natural bonds before marriage. There are those who suggest no kissing, holding hands, hugs, or anything physical. A century ago, couples were not even allowed to be alone together unless they had a chaperone.

Just because **you can handle** *certain things* **does not mean he or she can.**

The bottom-line is that you must know yourself and be both mindful and considerate of your mate. Just because *you* can handle certain things that does not mean *that your partner* can. Always protect each other, and never underestimate the strength of your flesh when it is left unchecked. Never bypass the safeguards that you both have put in place or exceed your partner's boundaries. Continue to show respect and restraint, no matter how deeply in love you are. As the Apostle Paul states in 1 Corinthians 7 verse 9, *"But if they cannot contain, let them marry: for it is better to marry than to burn."*

Lastly, if you have not already, make sure each of you is making the relationship and each other a priority. Marriage is where the two of you will become one, and courtship is where the process begins. This is the time to develop *teamwork,* truly. Start to create and execute goals together by including each other's thoughts and opinions in making decisions. This is where *you and me against the world* develops. Both courtship and marriage are for the *unselfish.* This may be a difficult task for those who have been independent for a while, but it is necessary.

ENGAGEMENT STAGE

At this point, you are not just marriage-minded, you are marriage-ready. Men, do not put a ring on her finger if you are not marriage-ready. Ladies, you should not accept the ring if you are not marriage-ready. This is the stage where you have already established if the person is the right one for you

Two people say I do.
A good yoke is established,
and a wonderful soul-tie is made.
Spiritual DNA collides
and produces one new person.
When done right with the right person,
in time it becomes a microcosm
of the marriage between Christ
and His Bride, the Church.

I *strongly* suggest holding off on the wedding until both of you can get sound, biblical marital counseling. I am not referring to the counseling where you meet with a preacher weekly for a month prior to getting married. For a lifetime commitment, this is not good enough. Connect with a seasoned counselor who will not leave any stones unturned. Make sure you both understand and agree on your roles and responsibilities in marriage.

Do not enter the marriage with unrealistic expectations. Not only should you talk about finances, but also develop a financial strategy that works for both of you. Talk about sexual expectations. Talk about child rearing. Talk about domestic responsibilities. Talk about conflict resolution. Talk about caring for parents when they are older. Talk about living arrangements and locations. Talk, talk, and talk, but make sure you also agree, agree, and agree on the most serious topics.

How Long Should the Engagement Stage Last?

In my opinion, engagements should be less than a year. Traditional biblical engagements (betrothals) were designed to allow enough time to resolve all financial matters between the two families and prepare for the wedding ceremony. Engagements were not designed for uncertain and insecure people who want to take their prospective partner off the market for several years until they've made up their minds about their future with them.

> **Engagements were not designed** *for* uncertain *and* insecure people *who simply want to take you* **OFF THE MARKET.**

Is It Ever Okay to Call the Wedding Off?

If you are within days of getting married but you are uncomfortable with the decision, please know that you are not obligated to say,

"I do." I can only imagine the pressure and embarrassment of calling the wedding off after paying for everything, and everyone has already responded to the invite. However, it is better to be embarrassed and in debt for a while than to be married to the wrong person.

I remember an engaged young lady who attended one of my courtship workshops. Although she was in love and ready to get married, the information she received enabled her to reassess her relationship. Later, the young lady told me that she knew her fiancé was not the one she should marry and had decided to cancel the wedding. Remember that it is never too late to make a wise decision when it impacts the rest of your life.

I cannot tell you the number of divorced people I have coached who tell me they knew they should not have married their spouse. They knew it was not right, but at the time, it was something they wanted. Make sure you are not pressured into getting married. If you are not ready, you are not ready. When your prospective mate really loves you, he or she will respect the time you need.

Lastly, as Christ Jesus so eloquently stated, *"And ye shall know the truth, and the truth shall make you free"* (John 8:32). Do not attempt to build your marriage on a lie or intentionally withhold secrets or valuable information from your soon-to-be spouse. If you do, the relationship will not last. At this point, you should both be an open book to the other.

My key takeaways
for this chapter

_____

_____

_____

_____

_____

_____

_____

_____

_____

_____

_____

_____

_____

_____

_____

_____

_____

Joyful Courters Tell All

∞

"I, like so many others, have had hurtful experiences with relationships. I am at a point in my life where I have had to deal with ME and make appropriate changes so I can heal and grow and live abundantly (that is really what God wants! I am so grateful I am able to receive, and I appreciate and glean from WISE counsel. Courtship vs Dating (CVD) uses and applies principles that are aligned with God's standards. As I am learning and growing, I recognize and appreciate the teaching, the word, the encouragement, the confirmation CVD's posts contain, and am able to apply them in my own life. Sometimes that is all you need. Great work, you are making a difference.

Thank you!"

~ Tara Dash

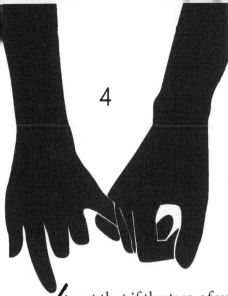

4

Courtship Success

I trust that if the two of you apply the following instructions to your relationship, you should both be overcome with the felicity of the results. In no way does this mean you will not experience conflict - you are two individuals coming from completely different households. However, when the following instructions are applied, they can produce amazing results!

Respect Each Other

Never lie to your partner. If you lie in the beginning, it will later permeate the structure of the relationship. Sure, sometimes the truth hurts, but at least you won't lose your partner's respect. Be transparent and do not hide things from each other. Every lie and every secret withheld, when discovered later, will create a greater divide between the two of you. Respect your partner enough to be honest with them. Trust him or her enough to know that what you share with them transparently will be handled fairly and covered in grace.

Make Your Relationship Other-Centered

Some would say that you should always put your happiness first. I do not have a problem with doing that *before* entering a relationship. You should strive first to be happy and healthy. However, once you are courting, your focus must shift from *me* to *us*. You must change your mindset. Seek ways to please and make your partner happy. You do not have to like everything you do for or with your mate but do these things anyway out of love. Your relationship requires you to be unselfish. Never forget that it is the small things you do over time that produce great benefits later.

Be Consistent

You must maintain the person you were at the beginning of the relationship. If you were attentive, caring, compassionate, God-fearing, responsible, respectful, and kind at the beginning, there is no reason those wonderful traits should change later. While courting, be intentional about maintaining a pattern. Consistency builds trust, and trust makes you dependable.

Apologize and Forgive Quickly

When you know you are wrong or your mate conveys to you that you have offended him or her, apologize quickly. The truth is . . . you may or may not have been in the wrong. However, the risk of destroying your relationship is not worth trying to prove how you may have been right. In the same manner, treat your mate's offenses toward you the same way and quickly forgive him or her. Learn how to make amends. Remember that when you truly forgive, you do not bring those offenses back up at a future date. Choose your battles wisely.

Embrace Your Differences

It is okay if your partner is not just like you—this is a good thing. Neither you nor your partner should ever lose your identity, regardless of how great the relationship between you two may be. Your partner does not have to like everything you like or participate in everything you participate in, and neither do you regarding him or her. Nevertheless, encourage your partner and let him or her grow. Support your partner's individuality and learn to embrace your differences. Allow those differences to improve your relationship, not destroy it.

Leave Past Relationship Failures in the Past

Maybe you were betrayed in your past. Perhaps by someone you thought you could trust and be with for the rest of your life. You must go through the process of healing before courting again. To give your new relationship a good chance of success, you cannot bring baggage from your past relationships into it. You must leave that baggage in the past. It is great to be wise in your new choices, but it is not okay to be overly critical. If you are already in a new relationship, just because your mate does something that reminds you of a past encounter, that does not mean your new partner should pay the price for it. Be honest with your partner and allow him or her to help you work through your feelings. I am sure God has given your partner just the right amount of grace for you.

Here are a few last points I want to leave you with, and you should understand them before engaging in courtship, and more importantly, before your amazing wedding day:

- Seek God to understand your purpose in life.

- Pursue a loving relationship with God first. He will show you how to love others.

- Be able to identify your core values and non-negotiables. This will help you tremendously in choosing your mate.

- Understand the importance of accountability partners.

- Understand the significance of love, honor, integrity, respect, and boundaries in relationships.

- Understand the significance of keeping a marital covenant. When you get married, do so with the mindset that divorce is not an option.

- Understand the purpose of marriage.

- Understand the significance of roles within a marriage.

MY KEY TAKEAWAYS
FOR THIS CHAPTER

_____

_____

_____

_____

_____

_____

_____

_____

_____

_____

_____

_____

_____

_____

Joyful Courters Tell All

"I met Rickey as a speaker at a women's conference maybe June or August of 2016; and ever since I've met him, his words have really been a source of inspiration to me. I have been using Rickey's courtship quotes and inspirations in my life, and they have made me change my process of dating and someone courting me. Rickey is a Great and Awesome speaker and Christ representor."

~ Lydia Smothers

5

COURTING TIPS, ENCOURAGEMENT AND ADVICE

*f*or those who are entering into a relationship, wanting to begin a relationship, or wondering whether a current relationship is the right one for you, I would like to offer this chapter to you. Through my social media pages and website, I have provided an abundance of tips, encouragement, and daily advice. I hope that you are able to take some of these to heart and that they will assist you as you navigate this journey.

COMMUNICATION PRINCIPLE

Communication is the key to a healthy relationship. Without it, you are left with assumptions and insecurities leading to frustration and confusion. Learn to speak to each other and not *at* each other. The survival of your relationship depends on this. Keep the lines open. Talk and listen but listen more than you talk.

BE AUTHENTIC

Be your original self. Authenticity will take you a long way. The right person will be inspired by your dreams and aspirations, but he or she will be more impressed with who you are. Whether you are exciting, corny, or quirky, you are just enough.

MAKE HIM FEEL SPECIAL

Ladies, show him you appreciate him. Allow him to lead and trust his judgment. Respect him and his decisions. Support him and cheer him on. Have a heart of gratitude for the things he does for you. Compliment him from time to time in the smallest things. Appreciate him and learn his love languages.

Woo Her

Gentlemen, your job is to woo her. You must put in the work, and you must do it consistently. Keep the communication flowing. When you are not around, check up on her with phone calls or text messages. Be chivalrous. Grab a copy of my book, *The Chivalry Project: A Black Book for Gents,* and put it to use. Make her feel special!

Be Approachable

Ladies, if you want to be approached, you must show yourself to be approachable. The person who gathers friends does so because he or she shows themselves to be friendly. If you intentionally avoid eye contact and conversation, then eye contact and conversation will probably not happen. If your disposition and demeanor show that you do not want to be bothered, most men will not bother you. Smile and sometimes say, "Hi." It is okay to be polite. This doesn't make you desperate, it makes you approachable.

LUST VERSUS LOVE

Lust will not allow you to wait, but love will. Lust will temporarily fulfill your appetite, but love will unselfishly satisfy for a lifetime. Lust is a mirage in a desert, but love is an ocean that never runs dry.

WHO YOU MARRY MATTERS

Your sanity, your finances, your health, and your destiny are all tied to the decision of who you marry. Choose wisely.

BE WISE AND FAITHFUL

A wise woman builds her house. A faithful man protects it. Your marriage requires both.

GUARD YOUR HEART

Guarding your heart does not mean building a fortress. A fortress doesn't allow anyone in; it also doesn't allow anyone out. Fortresses are great when God hides you for a season of preparation for your mate, but they are not so great when you are hiding yourself. Take your time to heal first. However, do not allow fears from past relationships to keep you from believing there is something better waiting for you.

WHO AM I?

If you do not know who you are (your identity), and you do not know why you are (your purpose), and you do not know what you are (your uniqueness), then what are you going to present to your mate when he or she shows up? Seek to discover yourself before you seek to discover your mate.

BE A PROTECTOR

Men, we have a responsibility to guard and protect everything God places in our care. One of the greatest pearls we have been commissioned to protect is our woman's heart. Let us do our best to affectionately care for it as if it were our very own.

Real Substance

Life will teach you that you can be enamored by looks and build a pseudo-relationship upon them, but it will never produce a great marriage.

It is fine to desire an attractive person but looks alone will not produce a great relationship. For that, you need someone with real substance.

Real Talk

Ladies: The best way to a man's heart is not through food. It is through honoring him, respecting him, and supporting him.

Gentlemen: You are not meant to sow your seed in everyone's field. Reserve yourself for your wife.

Ladies and Gentlemen: If your prospective partner cannot be faithful in singleness, there is no logical reason to believe he or she will do so in marriage.

RESPECT YOUR MATE ENOUGH TO PROTECT HIM OR HER

Physically desiring someone is one thing but attempting to pull him or her from God's presence is another. If he or she expresses to you the desire to wait until marriage before having sex, please respect the decision. If you say you love him or her, prove it by safeguarding what that person holds most dear. If you will not protect your partner in his or her singleness, how can he or she trust you to show respect in marriage?

INTIMACY IN COURTSHIP

Intimacy is not forbidden in your relationship, but it may be misunderstood. Some of the most intimate moments are the walks in the park, hand holding, and cooking experimental meals together. Have you noticed that I did not once mention *sex*?

THE PRECEDENCE YOU SET

The precedence you set or allow in your relationship will become a reality in your marriage. If you practice certain habits now, you will more than likely practice them later in marriage.

MARRIAGE IS NOT A MIRACLE

Saying, "I do," does not transform a sinner into a saint, a pathological liar into a person of integrity, or a cheater into the most loyal spouse in the world. We are who we are, and that is who we will be after the wedding day.

VISION IS NECESSARY

Gentlemen: God gave Adam vision and responsibility. He then formed Eve from Adam. Next, God brought Eve back to Adam to help him, not to support him financially or provide for him. A part of her duty in marriage is tied to your vision. You must give her a vision to work with.

Boaz and Ruth

When Boaz discovered Ruth, she said, *"Why have I found grace in your eyes, that thou shouldest take knowledge of me, seeing I am a stranger?" (Ruth 2:1).*

Ruth found grace, and Boaz found favor! That is what happens when there is a heavenly connection with a divine purpose.

He or She Is a Keeper!

When you have a partner who is faithful to you *because* he or she is faithful to God, who honors you *because* he or she honors God, and who loves you *because* he or she loves God, you have a partner worth keeping. Because all that he or she does for you emanates from his or her relationship with God.

Six Keys to a Successful Relationship

1. Never take your partner for granted.
2. Stay faithful. Remain steadfast and loyal to your commitment.

3. Learn the art of conflict resolution. This could save your relationship.

4. Never try to win a fight. You and your partner are not competitors.

5. Learn your mate's love languages and use this knowledge to best communicate with him or her. If you are not familiar with the concept, check out Gary Chapman's book, *The 5 Love Languages*.

6. Most important of all these tips: never leave God out. You will need His Wisdom and Guidance throughout the marriage.

MARRIAGE-MINDED

When you are serious about being in a relationship and marriage is at the forefront of your mind, you do not have time to be going out with ten different people or craving attention from people you do not even know. All you should care about is meeting the right one.

If you are crying over a relationship, losing sleep over it, losing your peace over it, and going broke over it, there is a good chance that relationship is not from God. Remember that His blessings add no sorrow.

What Are the Implications of Marriage?

- As the two of you become one, aside from God, you are your mate's top priority.

- You are united with someone whose purpose and mission in life aligns with yours.

- You are united with someone who prays for you, is quick to forgive you, and has the right amount of grace for you.

- You are united with someone who encourages you to become your best.

- You are united with someone who provides emotional and physical security.

- You are united with someone who is committed to a lifetime of marriage.

- You are united with someone who honors you, respects you, and allows you to be yourself.

- You are united with someone who laughs with you, cries with you, and heals with you.

- You are united with someone who sees all your faults and loves you anyway.

- Through mutual transparency and trust, this loving relationship enables you to be vulnerable.

- In all seasons of your marriage, you have a consistent friend, a lover, and a loyal confidant.

- When faced with life's challenges, you will never again have to face them alone.

PRAYING POINTS
FOR YOUR FUTURE WIFE

PRAY:

- That she will fall in love with God before she falls in love with you.

- That she will be a good wife and a good mother.

- That her desire and love for you will increase as the years go by.

- That she will be your biggest cheer-leader, always encouraging and in-spiring you to be your best.

- That she will be a woman of grace and dignity.

- That she will have the ability to man-age her finances well.

- That she will live in divine health and take care of herself.

- That she will love you enough to be honest with you even when you do not want to hear it.

- That she will lovingly support your decisions and pray about those she disagrees with.

- That she will revere you and willingly support your position as head of the home.

Until she comes, **pray.**

∽

Through wisdom is an house builded;
and by understanding it is established.
(Proverbs 24:3)

PRAYING POINTS FOR
YOUR FUTURE HUSBAND

PRAY:

- That he will fall in love with God before he falls in love with you.

- That he will be a good husband and a good father.

- That he will be faithful to God first, and then to you.

- That he will be a man of great humility.

- That he will be a spiritual leader in the home.

- That he will have the ability to manage his finances well.

- That he will live in divine health and take care of himself.

- That he will be a great listener.

- That he will have eyes for you and you only.

- That he will manage his home well.

Until he comes, **pray.**

A LETTER TO YOUR FUTURE SPOUSE

I am alone, but I am not lonely. I desire a mate, but I am not desperate. I know who I am, and I refuse to settle. Until we meet, I will continue to focus on developing me.

I refuse to give you someone who is broken, hurt, and damaged. I refuse to give you someone who will not love or believe they can be loved. I am not looking for you to fix or heal me. I am leaving that up to God.

My past has not been pretty. My present is much better. My future is even brighter. I am the sum of my choices, and I refuse to play the victim.

I just wanted you to know that while I may be waiting, I am not sitting idle. I am not waiting for you to arrive so I can work on becoming the best.

I look forward to meeting you. Until then, I am sure you are working on yourself too. See you soon.

A Letter to Your Future Wife

I know it appears that I am not coming, but please do not give up on me. The truth is I am searching for you even now and will find you.

Before the world began, God already knew that you would be mine, and that season is much closer than you think. In time, we will become a reality in spirit, soul, and body.

So, if you are becoming impatient, please do not. Until I come, please keep pursuing your dreams and always stay connected to God. And when I cross your mind, put in a prayer for me so that when we do meet, I will have become everything you have ever dreamed.

Forever yours,

Your Future Husband.

MY LETTER TO MY FUTURE SPOUSE

⬭

_____

_____

_____

_____

_____

_____

_____

_____

_____

_____

_____

_____

_____

_____

_____

_____

MY LETTER CONTINUED . . .

_____

_____

_____

_____

_____

_____

_____

_____

_____

_____

_____

_____

_____

_____

_____

_____

_____

STANDING AT THE ALTAR

Finally, when the moment arrives, and you are standing face-to-face at the altar with the greatest earthly gift your Heavenly Father could give you, the joy and delight should overwhelm you. The sheer magnitude of the moment may be expressed by the tears of happiness that flow from your eyes and begin their journey down your cheeks.

As you continue to gaze into the eyes of your best friend, the one that takes your breath away, it suddenly hits you. All the preparation was worth the wait and worth the process. Your heart sings as you joyfully repeat the vows that will offer your life, your hopes, and your dreams to be one with your partner, the one your heart deeply loves.

As excited as you may be regarding your big day, please remember that the wedding day is never as important as the marriage itself.

"Two are better than one; because they have a good reward for their labour. For if they fall, the one will lift up his fellow: but woe to him that is alone when he falleth; for he hath not another to help him up. Again, if two lie together, then they have heat: but how can one be warm alone? And if one prevails against him, two shall withstand him; and a threefold cord is not quickly broken."

~ Ecclesiastes 4:9-12

Courtship

Dear Heavenly Father,

I pray for every person who has taken the time to read this book. May it serve as a new standard for how they view and approach relationships moving forward. Let it be an answer to someone's prayer who desperately needs to break the cycle of bad choices, heartbreaks, and dead-end relationships. May it be a source of wisdom to those who lack it and knowledge to those who need it.

As Your children pursue relationships, may they always be reminded that their vertical relationship with You must always take priority over their horizontal relationships with others.

Open the eyes of those who are blind. Please give them discernment. Heal the brokenhearted. Calm their fears and enable them to love again. Cover and protect them in temptation. Hide them until Your perfect time. Keep them from becoming anxious and impatient. Let them rest in You, knowing that You will perfect and bring to pass that which concerns them, for it is Your desire to give us the kingdom!

In Christ Jesus' name, Amen.

MY KEY TAKEAWAYS
FOR THIS CHAPTER

_____

_____

_____

_____

_____

_____

_____

_____

_____

_____

_____

_____

_____

_____

_____

_____

Courtship

_____

_____

_____

_____

_____

_____

_____

_____

_____

_____

_____

_____

_____

_____

_____

_____

_____

_____

_____

_____

_____

_____

_____

_____

_____

_____

_____

_____

_____

_____

_____

_____

_____

_____

_____

_____

_____

_____

_____

Joyful Courters Tell All

∞

"Thank you for all your lessons on courtship vs dating. You have no idea how helpful your CourtshipVsDating Facebook page is. Keep on keeping on. We see it all the way in South Africa!"

~ Misha Solanga

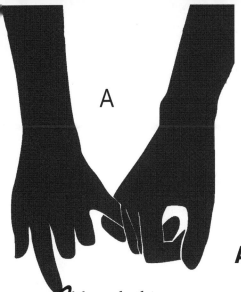

A

BEFORE YOU SAY "I DO" ASSESSMENT

*A*lthough this assessment section is near the end, it is of no lesser importance. The answers you give to the questions in this section will give you much-needed insight on the path that your current relationship will take. Please take your time and answer each question honestly.

If your answers confirm your current relationship, may God's favor and blessings be upon it, as well as your future marriage. If your answers are not favorable, and you realize this might not be a relationship that exemplifies God's best for you, please take the time to reflect and decide whether the relationship will continue.

What Are My Core Beliefs?

- Have I compromised, or am I about to compromise, my core standards and beliefs by entering a marriage with this person?

- Are we equally yoked?

Are We Better Together?

- Is my life truly better than it was before this person came into it?

- In what ways do our purposes align?

- Do we understand one another and how we each handle conflicts?

- Does this person inspire me to be my best self?

- Is there mutual support between us?

- What attributes make this person the right choice for me?

- Is this God's best for me?

'TIL DEATH DO US PART

- Is there anything I want to change about my mate?
- Can I live the rest of my life with him or her if that change never happens?

AT THE ALTAR

- Has my mate become my best friend?
- Can I confidently share my greatest joy as well as confide my deepest fears with my mate?
- Can I say I have been honest in all things with my mate?
- Is there anything in my past that I have not shared that could potentially create conflict in our marriage?

Joyful Courters Tell All

Been sharing your page with my UK Christian audience. Thanks for great advice and tips. We call it "The Love Therapy Page." lol

~ Kay Stern

Appendix

References

Cate, R. M., & Lloyd, S. A. (1992). *Sage series on close relationships. Courtship.* Sage Publications, Inc.

Jastrow Marcus; Drachman Bernard, *Betrothal* (אירוסין *in Talmudic Hebrew):* http://www.jewishencyclopedia.com/articles/3229-betrothal *King James Version Bible,* https://www.blueletterbible.org/

Lauritsen, Jason, *Relationship and Accountability,* https://jasonlauritsen.com/2018/06/relationships-and-accountability/, (June 29, 2018)

Macklin, Rickey E., *Real Talk Relationship Tips: A Biblical Perspective,* Copyright © 2012 by Macklin Publishers, LLC

Merriam-Webster.com Dictionary, Merriam-Webster, https://www.merriam-webster.com/dictionary/

Munroe, Myles, Dr., *Purpose and Power of Love and Marriage,*

Destiny Image Publishers; 12.2.2004 edition (January 1, 2005)

Shawn Grover, Shawn; Helliwell, John F., *How Life At Home? New Evidence On Marriage And The Set Point For Happiness,* Working Paper 20794, https://www.nber.org/papers/w20794, The National Bureau of Economic Research, (December 2014)

The Victorian Era England facts about Queen Victoria, Society & Literature http://victorian-era.org/victorian-era-court-ship-rules-and-marriage.html

Wu, Katherine. *Love, Actually: The science behind Lust, Attraction, and Companionship,* http://sitn.hms.harvard.edu/flash/2017/love-actually-science-behind-lust-attraction-companionship/

JOYFUL COURTERS TELL ALL

∞

"We both agreed to take the Courtship vs. Dating class to gain greater insight on the courtship process before getting married. Even though we both knew we were for each other, the class taught us what was required of both the man and the woman. As a result of the class, we both agreed to separate ourselves for a time to fast and pray for clarity from God.

We are now celebrating 13 years of marriage. Macklin's teaching on courtship is a must for all Christian singles and Christian couples who are seeking biblical principles to follow in a godly relationship."

~ Vincent and Dionne Bush

Joyful Courters Tell All

∞

Because of the marriages we witnessed growing up, by the time we were in our mid-20s, we had both resigned that marriage was not for us.

We couldn't believe God's design for marriage was two people living "miserably-ever-after" as was our experience both in and outside of the church.

We prayed and asked God to show us something different if marriage was what he wanted for us. God answered that prayer through Rickey Macklin's Courtship class.

Prior to meeting each other, we were two single Christians skeptically investigating this thing called marriage. Macklin's Courtship teaching offered a safe space, a Christ-centered framework, and practical tools to do so.

Courtship

The Courtship class helped us sculpt a clear mission and vision for what God wanted out of our single season which ultimately laid the foundation for a thriving single and, later, married life.

As a result of and during this course, we were able to do the hard internal work which lead to external (eternal) gains.

As the late Dr. Myles Munroe famously said, "When the purpose of something isn't known, abuse is inevitable." Knowing your vision and mission for this season of your life will only make discerning Mr./Mrs. Right that much easier.

~ Chandler & Kaneia Crumlin,
Celebrating eight years of marriage

About the Author

Rickey E. Macklin, founder of Courtship vs. Dating, is a highly sought-after speaker, known for his "Back to the Basics (B2B)" seminars, which are presented to groups of all sizes. If you are interested in having Rickey present to your group or ministry for your next event, please contact him at

CourtshipVsDating.com/speaking-request

Resources

Don't forget to check out
other products and services at:

 CourtshipvsDating.com

 CourtshipVsDating

 CourtVDate

 CourtshipVsDating

 CourtshipVsDating

And these books by the author

God's Whole Armor
Anointed But Not Ready
Daddy's Waiting On You
Real Talk Relationship Tips
6 Points To Optimizing Your Life
The Chivalry Project
Inspiring Moments

Made in the USA
Columbia, SC
02 December 2022

72514361R00067